INSIDE THE NFL

DENVER BRONCOS

by Charlie Beattie

Abdo & Daughters
MIDDLE GRADE NONFICTION

An imprint of Abdo Publishing
abdobooks.com

ABDOBOOKS.COM

Published by Abdo Publishing, a division of ABDO, PO Box 398166, Minneapolis, Minnesota 55439.

Printed in China.
052025
092025

THIS BOOK CONTAINS RECYCLED MATERIALS

Cover Photos: Michael Allio/Icon Sportswire/Getty Images (Bo Nix); Tim DeFrisco/Allsport/Hulton Archive/Getty Images (John Elway)
Interior Photos: Gregory Payan/AP Images, 4-5; Jason DeCrow/AP Images, 6; Focus on Sport/Getty Images Sport/Getty Images, 7, 26, 34-35, 41, 60 (top); Rich Graessle/Corbis/Icon Sportswire/Getty Images, 8; Kevin Terrell/AP Images, 9, 45; Charlie Riedel/AP Images, 10; Ezra Shaw/Getty Images Sport/Getty Images, 11, 61 (top right); Abdo Publishing, 12-13, 58; AP Images, 14-15, 19; Jerry Mosey/AP Images, 16; Bettmann/Getty Images, 17; Rich Gabrielson/Icon Sport Media/Icon Sportswire/Getty Images, 18; Denver Post/Getty Images, 20, 60 (bottom left); Bill Johnson/Denver Post/Getty Images, 21; Ed Andrieski/AP Images, 22, 36; Focus on Sport/Getty Images, 23, 33; Al Messerschmidt Archive/AP Images, 24-25; George Gojkovich/Getty Images Sport/Getty Images, 27, 32, 37; Lyn Alweis/Denver Post/Getty Images, 28 (top); Peter Read Miller/AP Images, 28 (bottom); Nate Fine/Getty Images Sport/Getty Images, 29; Vernon Biever/WireImage.com/AP Images, 30, 60 (bottom right); Eric Lars Bakke/AP Images, 31; Al Behrman/AP Images, 38; Rich Pilling/Diamond Images/Getty Images, 39, 61 (bottom left); George Rose/Getty Images Sport/Getty Images, 40; Don Emmert/AFP/Getty Images, 42; Kevin Reece/Getty Images Sport/Getty Images, 43; Jeff Haynes/AFP/Getty Images, 44, 61 (top left); Andy Lyons/Getty Images Sport/Getty Images, 47; Elsa Hasch/Allsport/Getty Images Sport/Getty Images, 48-49; Paul Spinelli/AP Images, 50, 55; Ronald Martinez/Getty Images Sport/Getty Images, 51, 63; Jack Dempsey/AP Images, 52, 61 (bottom right); Ric Tapia/AP Images, 53; Dustin Bradford/Getty Images Sport/Getty Images, 56; Tom Hauck/Getty Images Sport/Getty Images, 57; Elsa/Getty Images Sport/Getty Images, 59

Editor: Haley Williams
Series Designer: Laura Graphenteen
Production Designer: Laura Kuchar

Library of Congress Control Number: 2024948494

Publisher's Cataloging-in-Publication Data

Names: Beattie, Charlie, author.
Title: Denver Broncos / by Charlie Beattie
Description: Minneapolis, Minnesota: Abdo Publishing, 2026 | Series: Inside the NFL | Includes online resources and index.
Identifiers: ISBN 9781098296711 (lib. bdg.) | ISBN 9798384919230 (ebook)
Subjects: LCSH: Denver Broncos (Football team)--Juvenile literature. | National Football League--Juvenile literature. | Football teams--Juvenile literature. | American football--Juvenile literature.
Classification: DDC 796.333--dc23

CONTENTS

Linebacker Von Miller joined the Denver Broncos in 2011 and stayed with the team until the middle of the 2021 season.

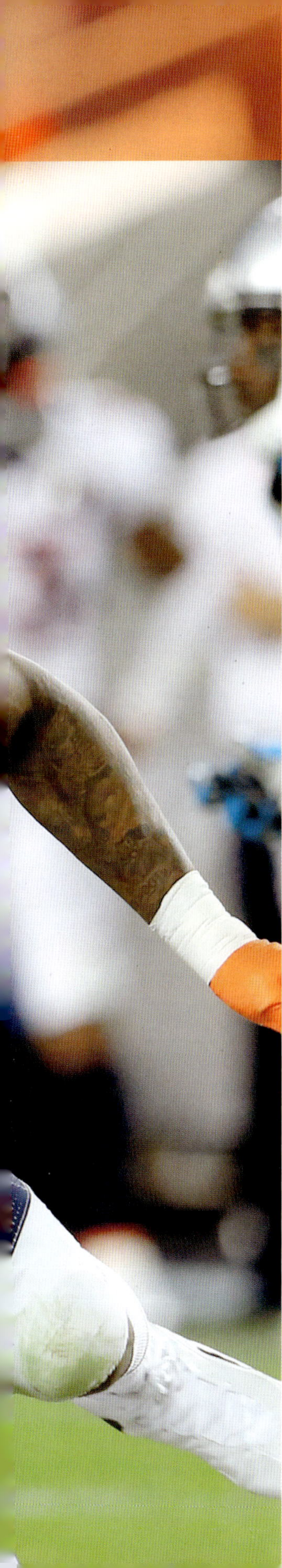

CHAPTER 1

MILLER'S THE MAN

At the snap, Von Miller exploded off the line. The powerful Denver Broncos linebacker locked his eyes on Carolina Panthers quarterback Cam Newton. Super Bowl 50 on February 7, 2016, was only a few minutes in, but Miller set out to make an early statement.

The Panthers faced third-and-10 at the Broncos' 15-yard line. Using his blazing speed, Miller flew around Panthers right tackle Mike Remmers and then bore down on Newton. The huge Panthers quarterback had no time to react. Miller was heading for an easy sack. However, instead of wrapping up Newton and pulling him to the ground, Miller threw both hands at the ball. Raking downward, he ripped it out of Newton's grasp as they both fell to the turf.

Quarterback Cam Newton, *left*, was selected by the Carolina Panthers as the top pick in the 2011 NFL Draft. The Broncos took Miller, *right*, with the second pick.

The ball bounced toward the end zone, and two Denver defenders scrambled after it with no Carolina players in sight. Defensive end Malik Jackson fell on the ball just as it crossed the goal line. The heads-up play resulted in a touchdown that put Denver up 10–0 about midway through the first quarter.

As the Broncos celebrated, Miller turned to the crowd behind the end zone and spread his arms wide. The fifth-year star from Texas A&M had been making big plays all season. Now he'd done it again, but this time, it was on the biggest stage in the National Football League (NFL).

SETTING THE STAGE

Super Bowl 50 presented an intriguing matchup. The Broncos were a storied franchise that had a pair of Super Bowl wins. In a quest for a third title, the team signed Peyton Manning, one of the NFL's all-time great quarterbacks, ahead of the 2012 season.

Quarterback Peyton Manning recorded just 2,249 passing yards and nine touchdowns during the 2015 season.

Over his first three seasons in Denver, the strong-armed Manning had lifted the Broncos' offense to a higher level. By the 2015 season, however, Manning began to show his age. Set to turn 40 just a month after Super Bowl 50, he was no longer the elite passer he had been during his younger years with the Indianapolis Colts.

On the other side, the dynamic Newton had the Panthers on the doorstep of their first championship. Standing 6 feet, 5 inches tall and weighing 245 pounds, Newton had a combination of size, a strong arm, and incredible mobility. Breaking down defenses with his arm and legs, Newton had earned Most Valuable Player (MVP) honors while leading the Panthers to the NFL's best record at 15–1.

This all presented an unexpected challenge for the Broncos. A few years earlier, they'd signed Manning hoping he would lead the way to a championship. Instead, the team showed up at the

Miller (58) forces a fumble in the first quarter of Super Bowl 50 in February 2016.

Super Bowl with a different game plan. The Broncos just needed their veteran quarterback to keep them in the game, while it was up to their ferocious defense to slow down the powerful Newton.

SEALING THE DEAL

Miller's big first-quarter play helped Denver jump out to an early 10–0 lead. But as the game unfolded, points proved difficult to come by. With just under five minutes to play in the fourth quarter, the Broncos were clinging to a 16–10 lead. They hadn't scored an offensive touchdown all game. Now they had to stop the Panthers, who took control of the ball at their own 24.

On third-and-nine, Newton dropped back to pass. Once again, Miller tried to sprint past Remmers, but this time, the Panthers' big tackle managed to get his hands on Denver's speedy linebacker. Miller continued to surge forward, though. Just as Newton

THE THIEF

Forcing fumbles was nothing new for Von Miller. The Broncos' star defender announced himself to the NFL in 2011 by knocking the ball loose from Oakland Raiders receiver Jacoby Ford on his first career play. In Miller's second season in 2012, he forced six fumbles. During his 10.5 years playing with the Broncos, he caused 25 fumbles and had 110 1/2 sacks.

Miller had 509 tackles during his career with the Broncos.

Miller, *left*, strips the ball from Newton's hand for a second time during Super Bowl 50.

cocked his arm to throw, Miller wrestled his left hand free and swatted the ball loose from Newton's hold.

A mad scramble ensued as soon as the ball hit the turf. A crowd of linemen fell on the ball, but it squirted out toward the Carolina goal line. Denver safety T. J. Ward raced in and recovered the ball at the Carolina 4-yard line just before Remmers could get to it. Denver took advantage by powering in for a touchdown. After the two-point conversion, the Broncos led 24–10. That score held up, and Denver won its third Super Bowl title.

Miller holds up the Vince Lombardi Trophy after the Broncos won Super Bowl 50.

Miller's performance was one of the best by a defensive player in Super Bowl history. He finished the game with six tackles and 2 1/2 sacks, and he also knocked down a pass by Newton. However, it was Miller's two incredible forced fumbles that earned him the Super Bowl MVP Award.

NFL TEAMS MAP

NFC

NFC EAST

- DALLAS COWBOYS
- NEW YORK GIANTS
- PHILADELPHIA EAGLES
- WASHINGTON COMMANDERS

NFC WEST

- ARIZONA CARDINALS
- LOS ANGELES RAMS
- SAN FRANCISCO 49ERS
- SEATTLE SEAHAWKS

NFC NORTH

- CHICAGO BEARS
- DETROIT LIONS
- GREEN BAY PACKERS
- MINNESOTA VIKINGS

NFC SOUTH

- ATLANTA FALCONS
- CAROLINA PANTHERS
- NEW ORLEANS SAINTS
- TAMPA BAY BUCCANEERS

AFC

AFC EAST	AFC WEST	AFC NORTH	AFC SOUTH
BUFFALO BILLS	DENVER BRONCOS	BALTIMORE RAVENS	HOUSTON TEXANS
MIAMI DOLPHINS	KANSAS CITY CHIEFS	CINCINNATI BENGALS	INDIANAPOLIS COLTS
NEW ENGLAND PATRIOTS	LAS VEGAS RAIDERS	CLEVELAND BROWNS	JACKSONVILLE JAGUARS
NEW YORK JETS	LOS ANGELES CHARGERS	PITTSBURGH STEELERS	TENNESSEE TITANS

Bob Howsam, *front left*, poses with the other owners of the original AFL teams in 1959.

CHAPTER 2

ORANGE SUNDAYS

THE DENVER BRONCOS HAVE LONG BEEN ONE OF THE NFL'S MOST popular football teams. But they may not have existed if it hadn't been for baseball. In the late 1950s, Bob Howsam was the owner of a minor league baseball team called the Denver Bears. Howsam wanted to get the Bears into the major leagues, so he expanded his stadium to fit big-league crowds. But when Denver was passed over by the baseball world, Howsam was left with a stadium too big to fill.

That's where businessmen Lamar Hunt and Bud Adams came in. Hunt and Adams had unsuccessfully tried to join the NFL in the 1950s. In 1959, they decided to start their own league to compete with the NFL. The American Football League (AFL) was born. Hunt and Adams approached Howsam about adding a Denver team to the AFL. Needing something to fill his stadium, Howsam agreed. Following a fan vote, he named his new team the Broncos.

The Broncos were a professional team, but they weren't a very good one in the beginning. The AFL had to fight for top players with the NFL. This meant paying out big contracts. Often, the top college players were selected in both the AFL and NFL drafts. In the early 1960s, the Broncos selected future Hall of Famers Bob Brown, Dick Butkus, and Merlin Olsen. However, with Denver unable to offer much money, all three signed with the NFL instead.

Quarterback Frank Tripucka (18) played in the NFL and the Canadian Football League before going to the AFL.

RAGTAG TEAM

The Broncos built their team with whatever players they could afford. Before the 1960 season, head coach Frank Filchock looked

In 1960, the Broncos, *in white*, took on the Boston Patriots in the first ever AFL game.

at his roster and didn't like the look of his quarterbacks. He asked assistant coach Frank Tripucka, who had recently retired as a quarterback in the Canadian Football League, to suit up. Tripucka became the starter right away.

Playing their first game on September 9, 1960, the Broncos beat the Boston Patriots 13–10. After another win in Week 2, the Broncos brought in Lionel Taylor, who had been a defensive back, tight end, and linebacker with the NFL's Chicago Bears the previous season. Impressed by Taylor's hands, Filchock moved Taylor to wide receiver. He quickly became Tripucka's favorite target.

In the Broncos' first season, Tripucka led the AFL in passing yards with 3,038. Taylor had a league-high 92 catches, despite playing in just 12 of the team's 15 games. However, after starting the season 4–2, Denver didn't win another game the rest of the year.

Tripucka and Taylor were excellent again in 1961. Taylor became the first receiver in pro football history to catch 100 passes in a season. However, the team finished with a 3–11 record.

GROWING PAINS

After two losing seasons, the Broncos weren't drawing many fans. The owners weren't sure the team could stay in Denver. But minority owner Gerald Phipps took over and promised to keep the team in town. The Broncos improved in the 1962 season. Under new coach Jack Faulkner, Denver won six of its first seven games, but then struggled down the home stretch to finish 7–7. The next year, Denver won only two games, and Faulkner was out early in the 1964 season.

The Broncos' struggles continued through the mid-1960s. In 1967, the team hired veteran coach Lou Saban, who had won two AFL titles with the Buffalo Bills. Saban transformed the Broncos. He fought for better practice facilities while also giving the team discipline and structure. In addition, Saban

BURN THE JERSEYS

The Broncos' uniforms during their first two seasons were considered some of the worst looking in football history. The uniform colors were brown and mustard yellow. When Jack Faulkner was hired as head coach in 1962, he ordered the jerseys and vertical-striped socks to be burned. Faulkner gave the Broncos their now signature orange-and-blue colors.

The Broncos wore throwback versions of their original uniforms in a game in 2009.

had help from a new star. For the first time, the Broncos signed their top draft pick. Although running back Floyd Little rushed for only 381 yards and one touchdown as a rookie, he soon became one of the most exciting running backs in football.

The Broncos also got the word out to fans that if they wanted to keep the team in Denver, people needed to show up to the games. The players, coaches, and staffers reached out to every potential fan they could. The city responded, and win or lose, going to watch the Broncos soon became the thing to do on Sunday afternoons in Denver.

HISTORY MAKER

Little was one of the big reasons fans came out to watch. Marlin Briscoe was another. At the time, there were no Black quarterbacks in professional football. Many people held a false, racist belief that Black players weren't smart enough to play quarterback, so teams often limited their Black players to other positions.

Running back Floyd Little rushed for a career-high 1,133 yards in 1971.

Briscoe had played as a quarterback for the University of Nebraska Omaha. But he was moved to wide receiver when he joined the Broncos in 1968. After several Denver quarterbacks suffered injuries, Saban turned to Briscoe in Week 3 against the Boston Patriots. The rookie nearly led a comeback victory. The next week, Briscoe became the first Black quarterback to start an NFL or AFL game.

Splitting time with veteran quarterback Steve Tensi, Briscoe helped lead Denver to its first win of the season, a 10–7 victory over the Cincinnati Bengals. Briscoe went on to start four more games late in the season. He led the Broncos with 14 touchdown passes and became a fan favorite. However, that marked the end of his time as a professional quarterback. Before the next season, Briscoe asked to be released from the team. He then signed with the Bills, where he went back to receiver and eventually made the Pro Bowl. In a career that lasted until 1976, Briscoe never started at quarterback again.

Quarterback Marlin Briscoe set a Denver rookie record with 14 touchdown passes in 1968.

HALF A LOAF

While Saban had helped the Broncos improve on the field, they were still far from being winners. The AFL and NFL merged in 1970, and the Broncos joined the new American Football Conference (AFC). Of the eight teams who founded the AFL, the Broncos left the league as the only one to never appear in the title game. When they joined the NFL, the Broncos still hadn't had a winning season.

Although the team didn't have a lot of success, the passionate Broncos fans looked for minor victories. The team had a chance for a big upset in Week 1 of the 1971 season. Facing the powerful Miami Dolphins, Denver was tied 10–10 late in the fourth quarter. However, Saban opted not to go for the win. There was no overtime during the regular season in those days, and the game ended tied. When asked about it after the game, Saban famously said, "Half a loaf is better than none." Angry Broncos fans showed up at the team's next home game

"HALF A LOAF IS BETTER THAN NONE."

—LOU SABAN

Head coach Lou Saban, *right*, talks with quarterbacks Steve Tensi, *left*, and Pete Liske, *center*, during a game in 1970.

two weeks later carrying half-loaves of bread. Saban resigned more than midway through the season after a 2-6-1 start.

TURNING THE CORNER

Denver's new head coach for the 1972 season was the energetic John Ralston. He inherited a team that now had talent. Little was coming off an NFL rushing title in 1971. Tough quarterback Charley Johnson had two strong receivers in rookie tight end Riley Odoms and deep threat Haven Moses. On defense, lineman Lyle Alzado, linebacker Tom Jackson, and safety Bill Thompson were the first pieces of what would become an excellent unit.

In the second-to-last game of the 1973 season, Denver clinched its first winning record. Little rushed for a touchdown, and Johnson

Linebacker Tom Jackson spent 14 years with the Broncos after joining the team in 1973. He was named to the Pro Bowl three times.

Tight end Riley Odoms (88) was named to the NFL's All-Pro team in both 1974 and 1975.

connected on scoring passes to both Odoms and Moses in a 42–28 win over the San Diego Chargers. While that game was on the road, Denver home games were jam-packed with orange-clad fans. The team had sold out every game since the start of the 1970 season. Game days in Denver were called "Orange Sundays," with fans encouraged to wear any orange clothing they had. The color lit up what was now Mile High Stadium, which held 50,000 fans.

Ralston crafted another winning season in 1974. By the end of 1976, Denver had finished second in the AFC West Division three straight years. But the team's records weren't good enough to make the playoffs. Meanwhile, a group of players wrote a letter to the owners asking for Ralston to be fired. The owners obliged, and Red Miller took over for the 1977 season. With a talented roster and a new head coach, the Broncos finally appeared ready to contend.

By 1977, Denver's Mile High Stadium was one of the largest in the NFL.

CHAPTER 3

ORANGE CRUSH

When the Denver Broncos took the field at Mile High Stadium for the season opener in 1977, they did so surrounded by a sea of orange. The stadium had been expanded again to hold 75,000 fans. It was full every week, and the team's rabid fan support was deemed "Broncomania."

New coach Red Miller had years of experience as an offensive line coach, and he had been an assistant coach during the Broncos' early days. Miller's players respected his toughness and fair-minded approach. Denver also had a new quarterback. Veteran Craig Morton came over from the New York Giants. Before that, he had played in Super Bowl V with the Dallas Cowboys. Denver players welcomed the experienced quarterback and embraced his leadership.

SHUTDOWN DEFENSE

Linebacker Randy Gradishar was named to the Pro Football Hall of Fame in 2024.

The Broncos opened the 1977 season with a 7–0 shutout of the visiting St. Louis Cardinals. The game was a preview of what the Broncos' defense was capable of. Up front, defensive ends Lyle Alzado and Barney Chavous harassed opposing quarterbacks. The linebacking group featured Tom Jackson and future Hall of Famer Randy Gradishar. In the secondary, safety Bill Thompson was named to the All-Pro team. Cornerbacks Steve Foley and Louis Wright each had three interceptions. Together, the Broncos' dominating unit was known as "the Orange Crush" as a nod to the popular soda brand.

The Orange Crush gave up more than 20 points only once in 14 regular-season games. After a 4–0 start, Denver traveled to Oakland to face the division-rival Raiders. The matchup was a huge test for the Broncos. The Raiders had won their previous 17 games, including the last Super Bowl. They'd been even more dominant against Denver, winning 26 of the previous 28 meetings between the teams.

The Raiders scored on an early touchdown, but then Denver took over. The Orange Crush intercepted Oakland quarterback Ken Stabler seven times. The Broncos also ran a fake field goal in the second quarter that resulted in a 25-yard touchdown pass to kicker Jim Turner. The Broncos dominated in the 30–7 win.

The Broncos entered the final game of the season with a 12–1 record. Despite a hard-fought loss to the National Football Conference (NFC)-leading Cowboys, Denver still ended with the best record in the AFC. The team was finally headed to the playoffs.

Cornerback Steve Foley played for the Broncos from 1976 to 1986. He set a team record with 44 career interceptions.

The road to the Super Bowl would not be easy, though. Denver hosted the powerhouse Pittsburgh Steelers in the divisional round. Pittsburgh tied the game 21–21 early in the fourth quarter. One of the Broncos' slogans that season was "The fourth quarter belongs to Denver." And the

Broncos fans hold up signs celebrating the team's success in 1977.

team lived up to it. Turner kicked a pair of field goals, and Morton threw a 34-yard touchdown pass to receiver Jack Dolbin to seal a 34–21 win.

The victory set up a third meeting with the Raiders that season in the AFC title game. Oakland once again took an early lead on a field goal. Morton responded two plays later by hitting receiver Haven Moses along the right sideline. Moses slipped

Wide receiver Haven Moses celebrates a touchdown in the AFC title game in January 1978.

a tackle and sprinted 74 yards for a score. It was the first of two touchdown connections between Morton and Moses in the game.

In the fourth quarter, Morton dropped back from the Oakland 12-yard line and threw a low pass to Moses in the end zone. The receiver made a diving grab to give the Broncos a 20–10 lead. Although Oakland scored late, the Orange Crush held up for a 20–17 victory. After the game, fans poured out of the stands to celebrate with the team as the Broncos carried Miller off the field.

CRUSHED

The Broncos had beaten the previous two Super Bowl champions in Pittsburgh and Oakland to reach Super Bowl XII. At the

The Broncos' fan section filled up the Superdome for Super Bowl XII on January 15, 1978.

championship game in New Orleans, they faced another one of the powerhouse teams of the 1970s in the Cowboys. Dallas's defense also had the catchy nickname of "the Doomsday Defense."

While both teams came out slugging, Dallas landed the bigger blows early on. Denver's first drive ended when Morton was sacked for an 11-yard loss on third down. On the Broncos' next offensive chance, the quarterback threw an interception that led to the game's first touchdown. Morton was then picked off again on the second play of the next drive.

By halftime, the Broncos had turned the ball over six times and trailed 13–0. The second half wasn't much better. Morton was hammered multiple times by Dallas's relentless pass rush. The veteran quarterback came into the game with an injured left hip.

Quarterback Craig Morton, *right*, struggles with pressure from the Dallas Cowboys' defense during Super Bowl XII.

He had spent most of the week before the AFC title game in the hospital due to the injury. Midway through the third quarter of the Super Bowl, Morton had to come out of the game. Backup quarterback Norris Weese didn't fare much better. The Cowboys sacked Weese twice, and he also fumbled the ball.

The Broncos lost 27–10. Although Denver fans knew the game was lost, they chanted "We love you" to the team throughout the fourth quarter. The chant continued as fans left the stadium. The defeat had not soured the loyal Broncos supporters. Superfan Tim McKernan later said, "We wanted to keep the Broncomania going. We didn't want it to die just because we'd lost the Super Bowl."

"WE WANTED TO KEEP THE BRONCOMANIA GOING. WE DIDN'T WANT IT TO DIE JUST BECAUSE WE'D LOST THE SUPER BOWL."

—TIM MCKERNAN

DENVER BARREL MAN

In 1977, Broncos fan Tim McKernan bet his brother he could get on TV if he wore an orange barrel and orange boots to a Denver home game. McKernan wore his barrel to almost every Broncos home game until health concerns forced him to stop in 2007. After becoming famous as "the Barrel Man," McKernan used his status to do some good. He auctioned off the barrel he wore to Super Bowl XXXII after the 1997 season, and then gave 10 percent of the proceeds to a women's shelter in his hometown of Gunnison, Colorado.

END OF A GOLDEN ERA

Denver repeated as AFC West champions in 1978 on the strength of the Orange Crush defense. The divisional round of the playoffs brought a rematch of the Broncos' regular-season finale against the Steelers. On that day, Denver fell behind 21–0, only to put up a furious rally before ultimately coming

Defensive end Rulon Jones had 73 1/2 sacks for the Broncos between 1980 and 1988.

up short in a 21–17 loss. When the teams met again two weeks later in the playoffs, the game was a blowout, with Denver losing 33–10. It was just the second time since the start of the 1977 season that an opponent had scored 30 points against the Orange Crush.

The Broncos started the 1979 season 9–3. However, the team lost four of its last five games. That included a 13–7 playoff loss to the Houston Oilers in which Morton was sacked six times.

By 1980, things were starting to come apart in Denver. The 37-year-old Morton threw more interceptions than touchdowns that season. Meanwhile, Alzado had left for the Cleveland Browns in 1979. He was one of several key defensive players Denver lost around that time. Despite rookie defensive end Rulon Jones picking up 11 1/2 sacks in 1980, the Orange Crush could no longer carry the team. Denver finished 8-8, and new team owner Edgar Kaiser fired Miller.

The new head coach was former Cowboys running back Dan Reeves. He led the Broncos to a 10-6 record in 1981, but Denver missed the playoffs. By 1982, the NFL's players felt the owners were keeping too much of the money that the league was making, so after two games, the players went on strike. The players' strike lasted 57 days and canceled eight weeks in the middle of the season. Denver never got going and finished 2-7.

Morton started three games, but the 39-year-old didn't throw a touchdown pass. His backups didn't fare much better. As Reeves and the Broncos looked forward to 1983, it was clear the team needed a new quarterback. Luckily, Denver was about to catch a huge break.

Dan Reeves, *front left*, won 110 games as the Broncos' head coach between 1981 and 1992.

Quarterback John Elway looks to pass during a game against the Los Angeles Raiders in 1983.

CHAPTER 4

ELWAY ALL THE WAY

The 1983 NFL Draft was known as "The Year of the Quarterback." Six signal-callers went in the first round. Leading up to the draft, however, Stanford's John Elway was the one every team wanted. The Baltimore Colts held the first pick of the draft that year. At the time, the Colts were a poorly run team with an unpopular owner. Elway said before the draft that if Baltimore selected him, he'd play professional baseball instead.

The Colts did take Elway, but the Broncos made a big move right after the draft. They traded their top pick, guard Chris Hinton, and two players for Elway. At the time, players didn't often question the teams that were about to draft them. Elway's power play wasn't popular in some circles. Terry Bradshaw, who was a four-time Super Bowl–winning quarterback for the Pittsburgh Steelers, even said that Elway should have stuck to baseball because the rookie didn't have the right attitude to win in the NFL.

THE DRIVE

Elway struggled early in his career. During his rookie season, he was outplayed by veteran quarterback Steve DeBerg. But in his second season, Elway won 12 of the 14 games he started. With his cannon of a right arm and extreme toughness, he soon became a fan favorite in Denver.

The Broncos reached the playoffs in each of Elway's first two seasons, but they failed to win a postseason game. That drought ended in 1986. After an 11-5 regular season, the Broncos rallied to beat the New England Patriots 22-17 in the divisional round. That set up an AFC title game on the

Elway threw so hard that he supposedly broke two of his teammates' fingers during his first practice with the Broncos.

Elway, *left*, threw for 244 yards and one touchdown during the AFC title game against the Cleveland Browns on January 11, 1987.

road against the Cleveland Browns. In a back-and-forth game, the Browns took a 20–13 lead on a long touchdown pass with just over five minutes to go. Then Broncos returner Ken Bell misplayed the ensuing kickoff and had to cover the ball at the 2-yard line.

Elway faced a 98-yard drive to tie the game. And he had to do so against an excellent defense and in front of 80,000 screaming Cleveland fans. As the Broncos stepped into the huddle, guard Keith Bishop joked, "We've got them right where we want them."

What happened next made Elway an instant legend. Over 15 plays, he marched the Broncos down the field. Right in front of Cleveland's rowdy "Dawg Pound" cheering section, Elway rifled a 5-yard touchdown pass to receiver Mark Jackson with 30 seconds left. Rich Karlis, who even in cold weather kicked without a shoe,

Kicker Rich Karlis (3) follows through on his game-winning field goal against the Browns.

tied the game with the extra point. Karlis then won the game in overtime on a 33-yard field goal.

"The Drive," as it is often called, is still thought to be one of the greatest drives in NFL history. And it helped send the Broncos back to the Super Bowl. However, Elway was upstaged in the big game by quarterback Phil Simms of the New York Giants. Simms completed 22 of 25 passes. While Elway threw for more than 300 yards and a touchdown, the Broncos lost Super Bowl XXI 39–20.

SUPER LOSSES

The following season, the Broncos once again won a dramatic AFC title game against the Browns. Denver then jumped out to an early 10–0 lead against Washington in Super Bowl XXII. Nothing went right after that, though. The Broncos allowed a Super Bowl–record 35 points in the second quarter. Washington won 42–10 as Elway threw three interceptions.

Receiver Ricky Nattiel (84) scored the Broncos' only touchdown in Super Bowl XXII on January 31, 1988.

After the 1989 regular season, the Broncos beat the Browns again in the AFC title game to reach Super Bowl XXIV. Denver was considered an underdog in the matchup against the San Francisco 49ers, who were the defending Super Bowl champions. Bradshaw, in previewing the game as a TV analyst, said that if the Broncos weren't careful, they could be down 55–3 by halftime.

Bradshaw was kidding, but he was nearly right. Elway completed only 10 of 26 passes and was intercepted twice. On the other side, Denver couldn't stop legendary San Francisco quarterback Joe Montana, who threw five touchdown passes during the game. Denver lost 55–10, which was the biggest blowout in the history of the Super Bowl.

Mike Shanahan had been an assistant coach with the Broncos in the late 1980s before returning as head coach in 1995.

THE HELICOPTER

The loss to the 49ers tied Denver with the Minnesota Vikings for the most Super Bowl defeats. While Elway remained beloved in Denver, other people wrote him off as a good player who folded in football's biggest game.

Running back Terrell Davis rushed for more than 1,000 yards in each of his first four NFL seasons.

The quarterback needed some help, especially after the Broncos reached the playoffs only twice in the next five seasons.

In 1995, owner Pat Bowlen hired Mike Shanahan as the Broncos' new head coach. The Broncos also added several key pieces to help create a winning team. The team's best offensive players that season were unlikely stars. Terrell Davis was a sixth-round pick in the 1995 NFL Draft. With his combination of speed and power, he immediately became one of the league's best running backs. That same year, Denver added receivers Rod Smith and Ed McCaffrey. Smith hadn't been drafted, while McCaffrey was a free agent who barely played during his time with the Giants and 49ers. Working with Elway, the two soon became stars in Denver.

Davis tries to maneuver around the Green Bay Packers' defense in Super Bowl XXXII on January 25, 1998.

Denver won the AFC West in 1996 but failed yet again in the playoffs. A year later, the 12–4 Broncos were a wild card. Elway, Davis, McCaffrey, Smith, and star tight end Shannon Sharpe led the way for one of the league's best offenses. The defense wasn't the Orange Crush, but Denver had a solid unit led by linebacker John Mobley and safety Steve Atwater.

After winning its three playoff games, the Broncos reached their fifth Super Bowl. They were considered an underdog against the defending champion Green Bay Packers. The hype before the game was built around two gunslinging quarterbacks, the 37-year-old Elway and Green Bay's superstar Brett Favre. But it was Davis who stole the show for Denver. Despite battling a severe headache, the running back rushed for 157 yards and three touchdowns.

Even with Davis's brilliance, Elway made headlines because of one play. With the game tied 17–17 and just over two minutes to play in the third quarter, Denver faced third-and-six at the Green Bay 12-yard line. Elway took off on a scramble, and as he approached the first-down marker, three Packers defenders converged. As Elway dived for the marker, he took a hard hit that spun him around. He landed hard but still converted the first down. "The Helicopter" run exemplified Elway's hard-nosed style of play. Even late in his career, Elway wouldn't shy away from a hit. Two plays later, Davis finished the drive with a 1-yard rushing touchdown.

Elway flies through the air after taking a hit from three Green Bay defenders in the third quarter of Super Bowl XXXII.

Davis's third touchdown came from 1-yard out with 1:47 left in the game. The score put Denver ahead 31–24. After the game, it was revealed that Green Bay had let Denver score in order to get the ball back with time to try to tie the game. However, the plan failed when Mobley knocked down a fourth-down pass with 28 seconds left, sealing Denver's win.

> **"THIS ONE'S FOR JOHN."**
>
> **—PAT BOWLEN**

Bowlen had bought the team a year after Elway was drafted. The Broncos' owner received the trophy on a stand set up at midfield after the game. Denver fans watched as he hoisted it above his head and dedicated the win to the team's longtime star. "This one's for John," Bowlen said to huge cheers.

Elway holds up the Vince Lombardi Trophy after the Broncos win their first Super Bowl title.

ONE FOR YOU

At 38 years old, Elway returned for a 16th season in 1998 but missed a handful of games with a rib injury. Davis made both Elway's and backup quarterback Bubby Brister's jobs easy. The running back became the fourth runner in NFL history to top 2,000 yards in a season. Davis also led the league with 23 total touchdowns, 21 of those rushing. The Broncos

Wide receiver Rod Smith, *left*, hauls in an 80-yard touchdown reception in Super Bowl XXXIII on January 31, 1999.

finished with the best record in team history at 14–2. After beating the Miami Dolphins and New York Jets in the playoffs, Denver reached Super Bowl XXXIII to take on the Atlanta Falcons.

Denver led 10–3 in the second quarter when Elway dropped back to pass from the Broncos' 20-yard line. He threw a bomb down the middle to Smith, who caught it as he streaked past the Falcons' secondary and raced untouched to the end zone. Elway and Smith had drawn up the play on the sideline just before taking the field, and it helped Denver take control.

With just over 12 minutes left in the game, Denver led 24–6. Elway drove the Broncos to the Atlanta 3-yard line. He took the snap and plunged forward, just barely crossing the goal line for another touchdown.

THE MILE HIGH SALUTE

During the 1997 season, Terrell Davis began saluting teammates after he scored touchdowns as a way to honor members of the military. The celebration caught on with the entire team. Throughout the Broncos' championship runs, Davis and his teammates celebrated big plays with what became known as "the Mile High Salute."

In the final minute, Elway was taken out of the game, and as he jogged off the field, he took off his helmet and held both arms high in the air. No one watching knew that it was his final game, as Elway didn't officially retire until four months later. After Denver's 34–19 win, the team's longtime star quarterback was named the Super Bowl's MVP.

Once again, Bowlen accepted the Vince Lombardi Trophy as Super Bowl champion. But this time, he had a new dedication. The beloved owner pointed to the loyal Denver fans who had supported the team through both good and bad times since the early 1960s and said, "This one's for you."

Denver owner Pat Bowlen, *left*, holds up the Vince Lombardi Trophy after the team won its second Super Bowl title.

Quarterback Brian Griese drops back to pass during a 1999 game against the Kansas City Chiefs.

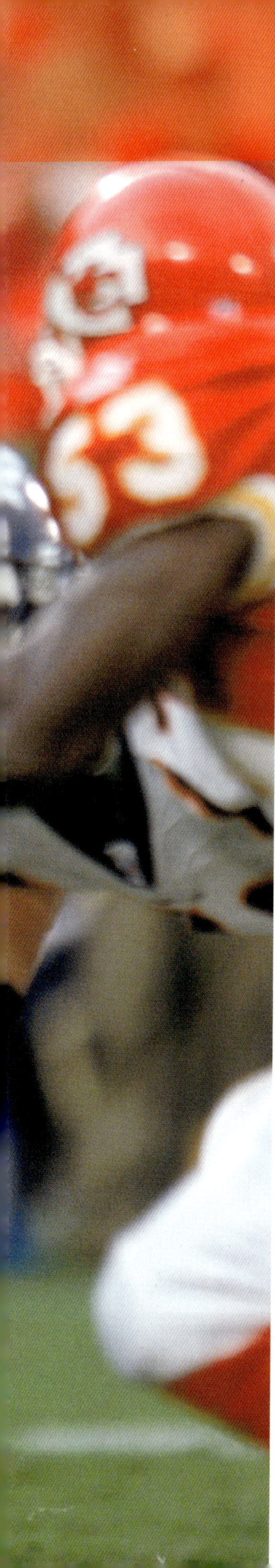

CHAPTER 5

MILE HIGH MOMENTS

THE BRONCOS ENTERED THE 1999 SEASON WITHOUT JOHN ELWAY FOR the first time in nearly two decades. But the team still had Terrell Davis, who was coming off an MVP performance in the 1998 regular season, and a promising young quarterback in Brian Griese. But in Week 4 of the 1999 season, Griese threw an interception. While trying to make a tackle on the return, Davis tore the anterior cruciate ligament (ACL) in his right knee. The team's superstar running back was done for the season. And his career would never be the same. Davis retired after the 2002 season after playing only 17 games in his final three years.

Coach Mike Shanahan's Broncos entered 2003 having reached the playoffs only once since their back-to-back Super Bowl titles. After letting go of Griese in the offseason, the team turned to veteran quarterback Jake Plummer. From 2003 to 2005, he led the Broncos to three straight winning seasons, including a division title in 2005 after the team finished 13–3. An excellent defense led by middle linebacker Al Wilson and cornerback Champ Bailey limited opponents to about 16 points per game.

Cornerback Champ Bailey had 34 interceptions in 10 seasons with the Broncos.

The Broncos faced a huge test in the divisional round against the two-time defending Super Bowl champion New England Patriots. New England star quarterback Tom Brady came into the game with a perfect 10–0 postseason record. But he couldn't get things going against the Broncos.

With the Broncos up 10–6 late in the third quarter, Bailey intercepted Brady at the Denver goal line. Bailey raced 100 yards the other way, but Patriots tight end Ben Watson chased the Broncos cornerback down and popped the ball loose just before Bailey crossed the goal line. The fumble went out of bounds at the 1-yard line. One snap later, Denver running back Mike Anderson smashed his way across the goal line for a touchdown. The Broncos went on to win the game 27–13.

The victory was Denver's first playoff win since January 1999. But the following week, the team fell flat. The Broncos were routed 34–17 by the eventual Super Bowl–champion Pittsburgh Steelers. Shanahan lasted three more seasons. He was fired after an 8–8 finish in 2008, but he left as the team's all-time winningest coach.

Running back Mike Anderson rushed for 69 yards and two touchdowns in the playoff game against the New England Patriots after the 2005 season.

AIRING IT OUT

As one legend exited, another returned to Denver. In 2011, the Broncos hired Elway to work in their office. His new job was to put together a winning roster. Denver's biggest issue was still quarterback. Plummer had been replaced by strong-armed rookie Jay Cutler in 2006. But he didn't turn out to be the answer. Neither did Kyle Orton or Tim Tebow, who followed Cutler.

In 2012, Elway brought in a future Hall of Famer to fill the spot. Peyton Manning had already enjoyed a legendary career playing for the Indianapolis Colts, including winning a Super Bowl. But after Manning missed the 2011 season with a neck injury, Indianapolis moved on, and Denver decided to sign the 36-year-old veteran. Manning immediately helped transform the Broncos into a dangerous offensive team.

Tossing deep shots to receivers Eric Decker and Demaryius Thomas, Manning threw for 4,659 yards and 37 touchdowns during his first year with the Broncos. The team had one of the top offenses in NFL history. And on defense, second-year linebacker Von Miller set a Broncos record with 18 1/2 sacks. The Broncos finished 13-3 and earned a spot in the playoffs.

In the divisional round, Denver hosted the Baltimore Ravens. With 41 seconds left in the game, the Broncos led 35-28 and had the Ravens backed up to their own 30-yard line. But then Baltimore quarterback Joe Flacco heaved an improbable 70-yard touchdown pass to tie the game. The Broncos ended up losing in overtime 38-35.

Although Peyton Manning played just four years with the Broncos, he left the team ranking behind only John Elway in passing yards.

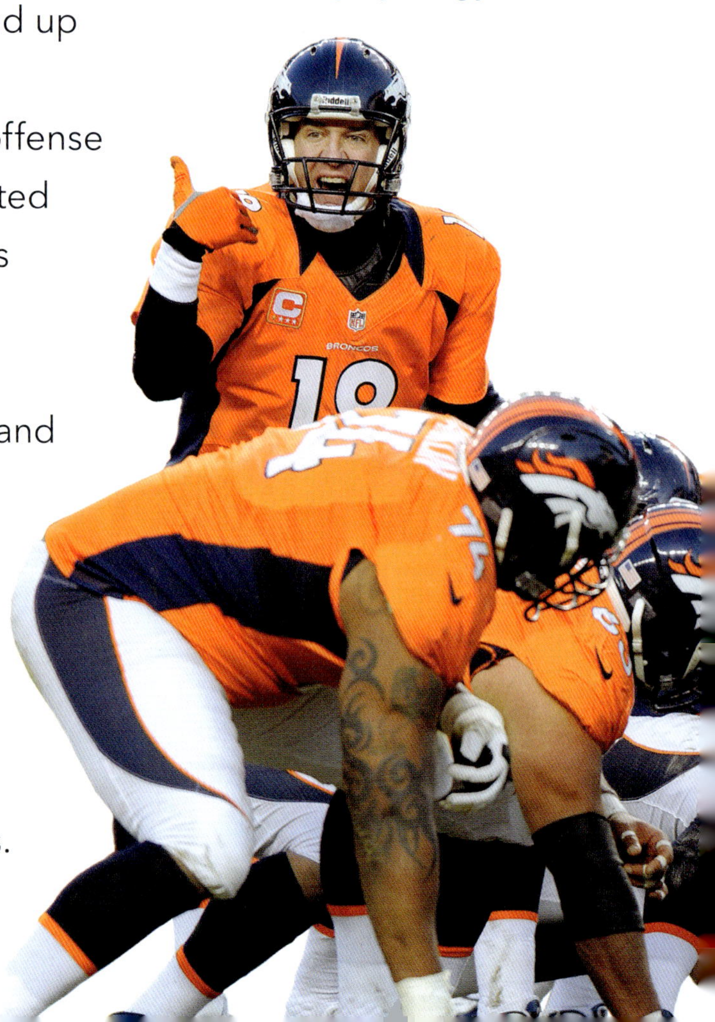

The next season, the Broncos' offense was nearly unstoppable. They started 6-0 while scoring at least 35 points in every game. On their way to another 13-3 record, the Broncos scored an NFL-record 606 points, and Manning set the league mark for touchdown passes with 55. After close wins over the Patriots and San Diego Chargers in the playoffs, the Broncos reached Super Bowl XLVIII on February 2, 2014, to face the Seattle Seahawks.

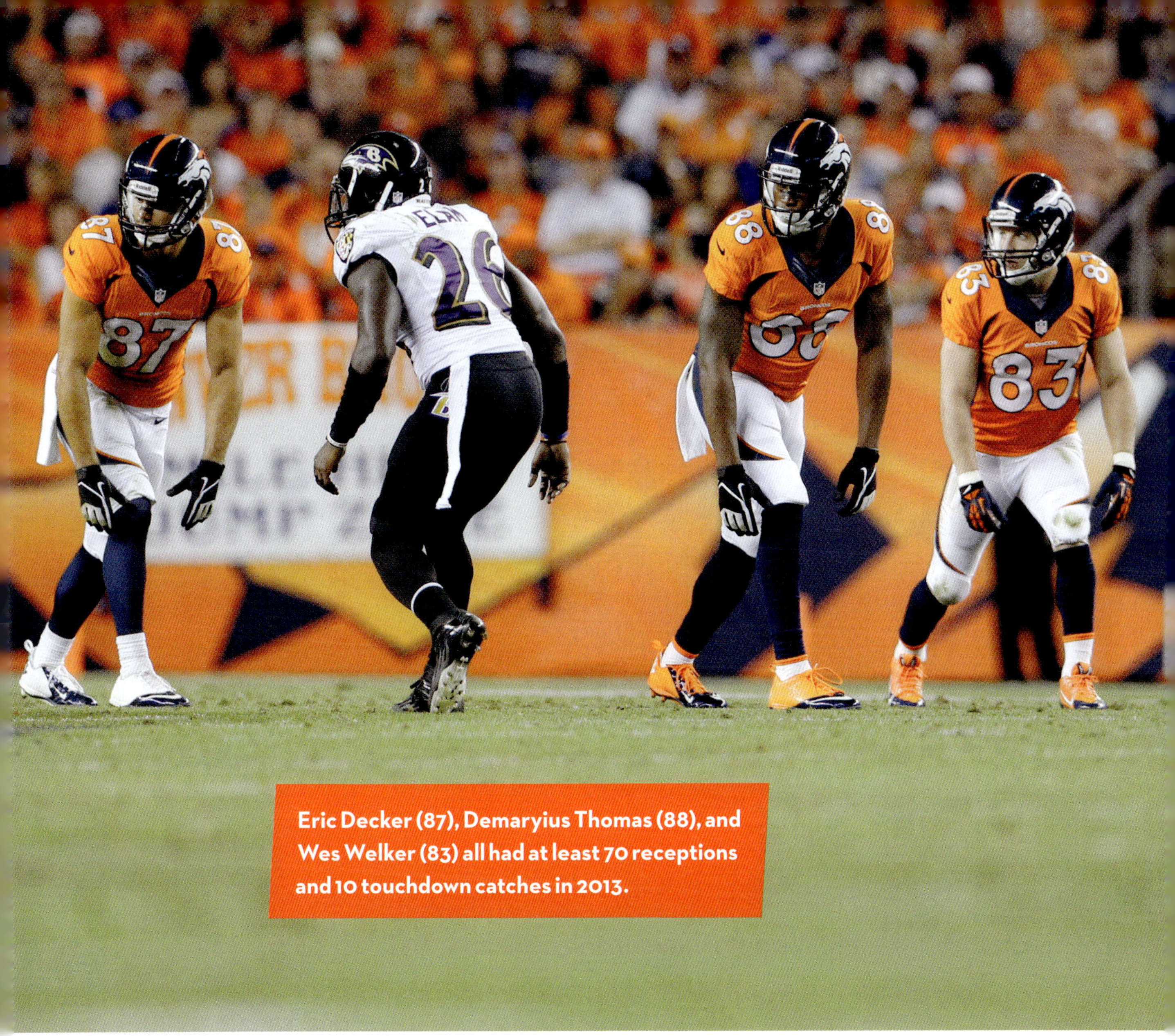

Eric Decker (87), Demaryius Thomas (88), and Wes Welker (83) all had at least 70 receptions and 10 touchdown catches in 2013.

The good feelings generated by Denver's season didn't last long in the Super Bowl. On the Broncos' first snap of the game, center Manny Ramirez launched the ball over Manning's head. Although Broncos running back Knowshon Moreno managed to recover the ball, he was tackled in the end zone for a Seattle safety.

That was just the start of a rough night for Denver. In a rare poor outing, Manning was intercepted twice, and he lost a fumble. The stunned Broncos were behind 36-0 before Manning and Thomas finally connected on a touchdown pass on the final play of the third quarter. With a final score of 43-8, Denver's historic season ended with a thud.

NO FLY ZONE

In 2015, Elway brought back another familiar face. Gary Kubiak had been Elway's backup quarterback for several years during their playing careers. Kubiak had also been the offensive coordinator for Denver's two Super Bowl wins in the late 1990s. He was considered one of the best offensive coaches in football. Elway hired him as Denver's new head coach.

However, the Broncos' strength came on the other side of the ball that season. At 39, Manning's arm power was fading. In 10 games, he threw only nine touchdowns against 17 interceptions. But the Broncos' defense dominated the NFL that season, allowing the fewest yards in the league. Miller and fellow outside linebacker DeMarcus Ware had a combined total of 18 1/2 sacks. The secondary of Aqib Talib, Chris Harris Jr., Darian Stewart, and T. J. Ward earned the nickname "No Fly Zone" for their abilities to shut down the opponent's offense. Denver finished 12-4, with nine of its wins coming by a touchdown or less.

A MILE HIGH VIEW

In 2001, the Broncos moved out of Mile High Stadium and into a new home. With the stadium having a corporate sponsorship, the team decided to call it Invesco Field at Mile High. The stadium has changed names several times since then, but it has always included "Mile High" as a tribute to the old stadium and to the city of Denver sitting 5,280 feet (1,610 m) above sea level.

In the divisional round, the Broncos looked as though they might be on the wrong side of another tight game. With 10 minutes to go, Denver trailed the Steelers 13–12. During a Pittsburgh drive, Broncos cornerback Bradley Roby forced a fumble that Ware recovered at the Denver 35. The offense backed up the turnover with a 13-play drive that took nearly seven minutes off the clock. Running back C. J. Anderson finished it off with a 1-yard touchdown run. Manning and Thomas connected on the two-point conversion to put the Broncos up for good. They eventually won 23–16.

Cornerback Chris Harris Jr. made the Pro Bowl four times during his nine years with the Broncos.

The Broncos hosted the Patriots in the AFC title game. The contest was billed as perhaps the last matchup between Brady and Manning, who had been battling for AFC titles since 2001. Manning tossed a pair of touchdown passes to tight end Owen Daniels, but the defense once again carried Denver. The Broncos sacked Brady four times and intercepted him twice, with Miller having 2 1/2 sacks and an interception.

However, the Patriots had a chance to tie the game late. With 12 seconds left, New England scored to cut Denver's lead to 20–18.

The Patriots then went for a two-point conversion to try to tie the game. Brady fired a pass over the middle, but Talib knocked it away at the goal line to preserve the Broncos' conference championship.

Miller continued his dominant play against the Carolina Panthers in Super Bowl 50. The linebacker had 2 1/2 of Denver's six sacks against league MVP Cam Newton and forced a pair of fumbles. Miller's second forced fumble set the Broncos up at the Carolina 4-yard line. Anderson put the 24–10 victory away with a 2-yard touchdown run with 3:13 left. It was Denver's only offensive touchdown of the game.

Tight end Owen Daniels, *right*, catches his second touchdown pass in the AFC title game against the New England Patriots in January 2016.

This time, Elway was the one who accepted the trophy on the victory stand. Longtime owner Pat Bowlen had recently been diagnosed with Alzheimer's disease, a brain disorder that affects people's thinking skills and memory. Bowlen was one of the most popular

Elway holds up the Vince Lombardi Trophy after the Broncos win Super Bowl 50 in February 2016.

owners in NFL history. Elway held the trophy high and remembered Bowlen's dedication from two decades earlier. "This one's for Pat," Elway said.

"THIS ONE'S FOR PAT."

—JOHN ELWAY

REBUILDING

Super Bowl 50 was the last game of Manning's career. The Broncos once again had to replace a legendary quarterback. In 2016, the team finished 9–7 but fell short of the playoffs. Kubiak resigned after the season for health reasons.

Between 2017 and 2022 the Broncos had a different starting quarterback each season. The team also went through four head coaches. Before the 2022 season, Denver brought in quarterback Russell Wilson, who had been Seattle's starter when the Seahawks

BRONCOS TROPHY CASE

SUPER BOWL CHAMPIONSHIPS: 3

Super Bowl XXXII – January 25, 1998
Super Bowl XXXIII – January 31, 1999
Super Bowl 50 – February 7, 2016

CONFERENCE CHAMPIONSHIPS: 8

1977, 1986, 1987, 1989, 1997, 1998, 2013, 2015

DIVISION TITLES: 15

AFC West: 1977, 1978, 1984, 1986, 1987, 1989, 1991, 1996, 1998, 2005, 2011, 2012, 2013, 2014, 2015

All stats are through the 2024 season.

routed Denver in Super Bowl XLVIII. However, in two seasons with the Broncos, Wilson struggled to produce.

After finishing the 2023 season with a losing record for the seventh season in a row, Denver started over again. Head coach Sean Payton, a former Super Bowl winner with the New Orleans Saints, drafted rookie Bo Nix as the team's new quarterback. While Nix struggled in his first few starts, he eventually thrived in Payton's system.

The rookie helped Denver stay in playoff contention heading into Week 18. Facing the defending champion Kansas City Chiefs, Nix threw for 321 yards and four touchdowns. With a 38–0 win, the Broncos were headed to the postseason for the first time since 2015. Even though the Buffalo Bills overwhelmed Denver 31–7 in the wild-card round, it looked as though the Broncos had finally found the franchise quarterback they'd been searching for.

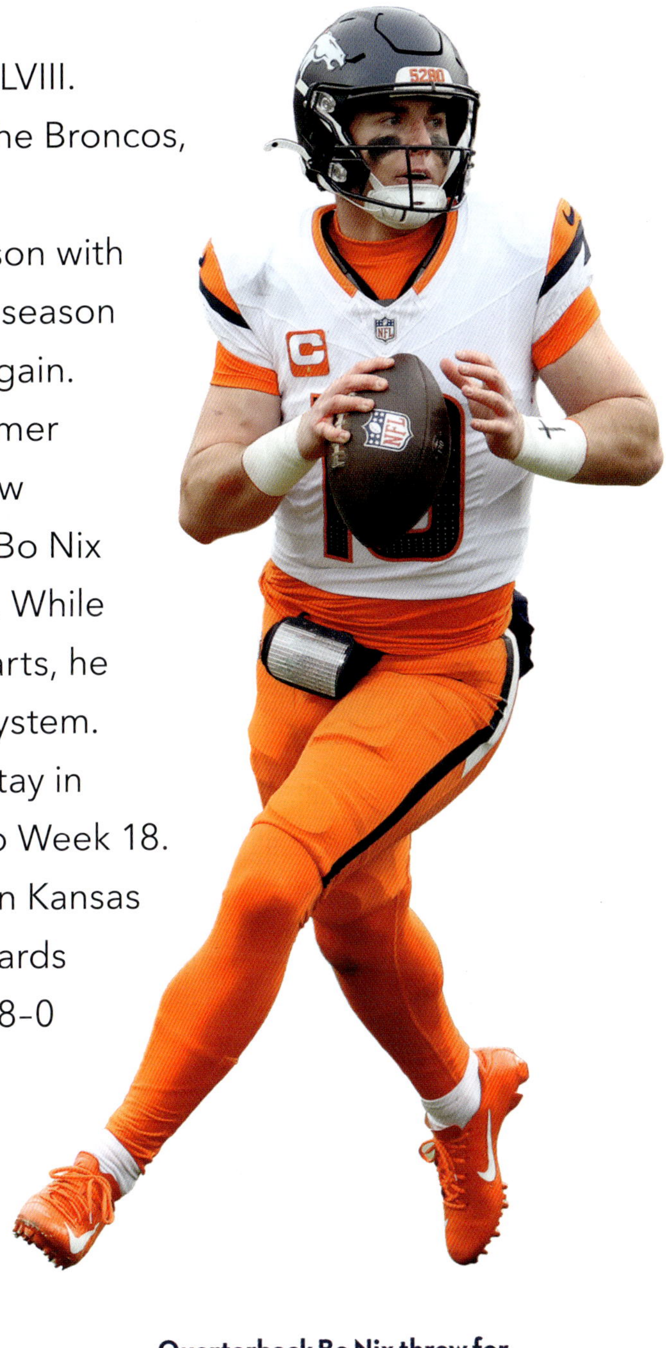

Quarterback Bo Nix threw for 3,775 yards and 29 touchdowns during the 2024 season.

TIMELINE

1960
The Broncos are founded in Denver as part of the new AFL.

1961
Denver's Lionel Taylor becomes the first receiver to ever catch 100 passes in a season.

1968
Marlin Briscoe becomes the first Black player to start as quarterback in either the AFL or NFL.

1973
The Broncos record a winning season for the first time in team history.

1978
Denver plays in Super Bowl XII on January 15 but loses 27-10 to the Dallas Cowboys.

1983
The Broncos trade for rookie quarterback John Elway.

1987
Elway leads "the Drive" as the Broncos defeat the Cleveland Browns in the AFC title game on January 11.

1988
On January 31, Denver loses the Super Bowl for the second year in a row.

1990
On January 28, the Broncos lose 55-10 in Super Bowl XXIV, tying them for the most Super Bowl losses.

1998
Denver defeats the Green Bay Packers 31-24 in Super Bowl XXXII on January 25.

1999
In his final game, Elway leads the Broncos to their second straight Super Bowl title on January 31.

2012
The Broncos sign star quarterback Peyton Manning.

2016
Led by Von Miller, Denver defeats the Carolina Panthers 24-10 in Super Bowl 50 on February 7.

2024
Rookie quarterback Bo Nix leads Denver to its first playoff berth in nine seasons.

GLOSSARY

comeback–a big rally after falling behind.

draft–a system that allows teams to acquire new players coming into a league.

dynamic–energetic and exciting; in sports, usually referring to an athlete with one or more outstanding skills.

franchise–an entire sports organization.

free agent–a player who is not signed to a team.

merge–join with another to create something new, such as a company, a team, or a league.

minority owner–someone who owns a small percentage of a team.

players' strike–a work stoppage due to a disagreement between players and their employers (teams) about things such as working conditions or wages.

resign–to leave a job.

retire–to end one's career.

rival–an opponent with whom a player or team has a fierce and ongoing competition.

rookie–a professional athlete in his or her first year of competition.

sack–a tackle of the quarterback behind the line of scrimmage before he can pass the ball.

safety–a score of two points for a team when its opponent is unable to advance the ball out of its own end zone.

secondary–the defensive players–cornerbacks and safeties–who start the play farthest from the line.

two-point conversion—an option for teams that have scored a touchdown to try a running or passing play from the 2-yard line for two points, instead of kicking for one point.

underdog—the person or team that is not expected to win.

upset—an unexpected victory by a supposedly weaker team or player.

veteran—someone who has played for many years.

wild card—a team that makes the playoffs even though it did not win its division.

ONLINE RESOURCES

Booklinks
NONFICTION NETWORK
FREE! ONLINE NONFICTION RESOURCES

To learn more about the Denver Broncos, please visit **abdobooklinks.com** or scan this QR code. These links are routinely monitored and updated to provide the most current information available.

INDEX